MY SMART-BOOK ON
MARKETING & SALES

THE CREATIVE MARKETING GUIDE FOR BUSY ENTREPRENEURS

Damilare Fakorede

Copyright © 2018 by Damilare Fakorede

Cover design by Damilare Fakorede

Edited by Adams Olashile

MY SMART-BOOK™ is a registered trademark of ICI CONSULTING. All rights reserved.

No part of this book may be reproduced in any form or by any electronic or mechanical means including information storage and retrieval systems—except in the case of brief quotations embodied in critical articles or reviews—without permission in writing from its publisher, ICI CONSULTING.

This publication is designed to provide accurate and authoritative information in regard to the subject matter covered. It is sold with the understanding that the material is meant for educational purposes only. If legal advice or other expert assistance is required, the services of a competent professional person should be sought

All brand names and product names used in this book are trademarks, registered trademarks, or trade names of their respective holders. ICI CONSULTING is not associated with any product or vendor in this book.

ISBN: 9781790693238

ICI CONSULTING
Info.iciconsulting@gmail.com
(+234) 814-009-2551

MY SMART-BOOK ON MARKETING AND SALES:
THE CREATIVE MARKETING GUIDE FOR BUSY ENTREPRENEURS

By
DAMILARE FAKOREDE
Author and Co-founder ICI Consulting

To my mentor, Christopher King, for his wisdom and faith.

To my late sister, Eniola Fakorede, Love always and forever!

CONTENTS

PRELUDE
WHY MY SMART-BOOK ON MARKETING AND SALES?

1. THE ESSENTALS

Marketing and Sales: What You Should Know

Types of Marketing

Why Marketing

It all starts with a plan

A quick 5-point draft

Start now!

2. YOUR UNIQUE VALUE PROPOSITION

Defining your Unique Value Proposition

What are you really selling?

Differentiate: Don't be among "the Many"

3. CUSTOMERS

It's all about the Customer

Types of customers

How well do you know your customers?

Attracting customers

Satisfying customers

Retaining customers

A word on Customer Relationship

4. THE MARKETING EDGE

Invest in Digital Marketing

Adopt quality Promotional Materials

Don't stop improving your business

Leverage your strengths

Getting the Best Returns on Your Ads and Marketing Campaigns

FINAL WORDS

ABOUT ICI

PRELUDE

In today's highly competitive and dynamic business atmosphere, Marketing is no longer an optional engagement. It is a necessity. Businesses, especially smaller ones are increasingly finding it hard to compete successfully. This has forced many business-owners to rethink their marketing strategies.

Of all business practices, Marketing, I believe, is the most important. This is primarily because not only does marketing **drive** your business, it also **position** you to compete effectively in the marketplace.

It is important to note that marketing isn't (and should never be) a one-time event. Rather, it should be a part of your everyday business routine. Understanding this simple truth is important to the long-term success of your business. This is why even big names like Facebook and Apple still dedicate a huge fraction of their revenue to marketing.

In "MY SMART-BOOK ON MARKETING AND SALES: THE CREATIVE MARKETING GUIDE FOR BUSY ENTREPRENEURS" you'll learn the essentials of Marketing and Sales, Hands-on, Practical and Ready-to-use ideas that can be applied to your business to get results immediately.

MY SMART-BOOK ON MARKETING AND SALES | DAMILARE FAKOREDE

The thoughts I'd be sharing can be applied across different kinds of businesses – Online or local Retail, Personal Service Firms, Auto-dealerships and several other areas.

This book will help you improve your marketing strategies, increase your sales and ultimately grow your business. I'll introduce techniques to help you make the most of your marketing strategy and turn your marketing plan into a system that can produce reliable and predictable results every time. In essence, it'll put your marketing efforts on autopilot so you can have more time to focus on other important areas.

In this book we'll explore four important areas:
- The essentials of Marketing and Sales
- Defining and leveraging your unique value proposition;
- Customers;
- Attracting. Satisfying and Keeping them;
- The Marketing Edge

Now those are pretty basic stuff right? Yeah. But guess what – as simple as these ideas are, only a few business owners know them. And even fewer apply them!

WHY MY SMART-BOOK ON MARKETING AND SALES?

Here are a few reasons why I think you should read this book.

It's Smart!

The book is concise, simple, straightforward, practical and applicable. In essence, the ideas you get from this book can be applied immediately to produce the results your desire to see in your business. It's written in simple everyday language and an easy to read manner. You don't necessarily have to start from the first page. You can quickly scan through and identify the subject that's most important to you at the moment.

You Can Sell More

No matter what your current sales level is, you can sell MORE! You shouldn't think because you're getting so many sales now things will always be this way. That'd be naive. Things change. Markets, especially, change every now and then. And if you're satisfied with the results you're currently getting in your business, I want to challenge you, don't make the sky your limit. There's an entire Universe out there! Shoot for higher results. Work hard at it. And I assure you, they'll come!

Don't think the sky is your limit. There's an entire Universe out there!

This Book Will Save You Time and Money

Instead of just getting needlessly frustrated and waste precious time worrying over what you **can** change, it'd be a better idea to invest some time in this book and learn what might save you some money and time. So, rather than complaining or grumbling over what you can change, just take a step to solve the problem - read the book, get the idea, apply it to your business and be happy.

You see, the harsh truth is that most businesses fail in the first few years of starting them, especially small businesses. Many fail at the very first year. One of the reasons for this failure is inadequate knowledge - of the product or service, the market and other important factors. That's why some 'experts' often advise entrepreneurs to do a SWOT analysis before starting any venture. However, I believe anyone can build a successful business if they can get the right information and be willing to work hard at it.

•••

People everywhere sell things; small, medium or large scale. So the profit you make isn't necessarily about what you sell, how large or small but **how much** you sell.

"Just another Marketing book?" that's what I heard someone say when I told them about this book. But guess what... It's not "just another marketing book". It is probably the 'Smartest' one you'll find online these days. Well, I'm not saying it's the smartest because it's got the latest and trending intellectual facts or the most recent Marketing jargon. It is Smart because it has the most important detail you'll need to take your business to the next level, and that, in just a few pages!

So many business owners, small or medium, are quite busy and they don't have the time to get their heads around the intimidating plethora of books available on Marketing and Sales today. So, if that describes your situation, this book is just what you need. This book isn't just for business owners. Salespeople and executives will also find the ideas very useful.

This book is the "Start here" book when you're interested in taking your small or medium business to the next level by improving your Sales and Marketing. The contents are practical, simple and straightforward, written in everyday language such that you can apply it to your own business almost immediately.

Finally, I'm glad you have this book in your hands. It's the greatest privilege ever, to be able to share valuable information with you. I encourage you to read it carefully and apply the suggestions, share it with your friends and colleagues who might need it. Also, feel free to leave a comment or review on my blog – www.damilarefakorede.com.

Now, get your notebook and enjoy this smart, fun and challenging journey to improving your business.

Damilare Fakorede
Author and Co-founder, ICI Consulting

1. THE ESSENTALS

Before we delve into the concepts we'll be discussing throughout this book, it is important to first understand the basics of Marketing and Sales. As said earlier, I won't be pushing any jargon to your face at all. It'll be simple and straightforward.

Marketing and Sales: What You Should Know

So what is marketing? Often, when asked this question people picture a man or woman in the streets, markets or stores who's always trying to push a product they don't need to their face. Some even recount an annoying call they received one midnight to buy a service they knew nothing about. We remember that sweet-mouthed man or woman in the electronic store who just wants to make the sale no matter what. All sorts of ideas come to mind when we think of this subject.

However, for simplicity's sake, I'd like to describe Marketing as the processes and means businesses employ to create value for customers in form of a unique offering that meets their needs so as to capture value back from the customers.

Marketing is the process and ways you employ to present your product or service to a customer, new or existing, for whom it is specifically designed to satisfy, so as to get the needed response - Sales.

In essence, the reason you're marketing is basically to get your product or service to someone that needs it and can actually pay for it. Sales is one of the most debated yet one of the least understood subjects in business. Many seem to have an idea what it's really about.

If you run a Google search right now on the word "sales", you'll get thousands of entries. That's how much sales has been discussed even on the internet. You can check in your local library and you'll see the several volumes of books available on the subject.

Sales, in the simplest terms is the exchange of goods and services for another form of value or commodity. It is the act of selling.

However, in a broader perspective, we all sell something. While some people are really fulltime salespeople some of us sell indirectly. We sell services, ideas and many other intangible things. Do you realize that whenever you try to persuade, influence or convince rather than force someone to do something you're actually selling? Whether you're trying to raise volunteers for your campaign, get people to vote you in an election, get investors to fund your business, get your kids to listen to you, make your boss understand that you need the raise, anytime you try to get others to buy into your idea or part with something valuable to them you're really Selling at that time. Now you should see that Sales isn't really as bad as many make it to be. I wonder how our lives would be without sales. Essentially, the ultimate reason for marketing, especially in business, is Sales.

Marketing is about Relationships. You're in a relationship with customers – to create and deliver Value for and to them. The ultimate reason for Marketing is to solve problems and create solutions for customers. From this perspective, you'll see that Marketing doesn't have to be about cheating ignorant customers with gimmicks and schemes. It's not a zero-sum enterprise. Rather it is a win-win situation – The customer is satisfied and you get paid.

Types of Marketing

There are several types of Marketing. A search query on Google will readily confirm the numerous and confounding categories there are. Here's a few of them:

- Direct marketing
- Indirect marketing
- Relationship marketing
- Viral marketing
- Word-of-mouth marketing
- Digital marketing
- Guerilla marketing
- CTA or Call-to-action marketing
- Transactional marketing and so many others too numerous to identify.

Why Marketing?

Someone might ask "Why do I have to market my product or service?" You even hear some say things like "I have a great product", "my service is excellent", "people love me so they'll always buy from me" and many other statements like that. But business is more than having a nice product. Neither is it about people liking you or not, at least in most cases. Here, cash is always KING! Without Marketing, there are little or no sales; no sales no profit, no profit, no Business!

Good Marketing is very important for the success of any business. Even nonprofits engage in some form or marketing. I would illustrate this simple truth with these thoughts:

Good Products + Poor Marketing = Poor results

Great Products + Average Marketing = Average results

Great Products + Great Marketing = Outstanding results

Again, Marketing is very important the success of your business both in the short and long terms. That's why even large and successful businesses still invest millions of dollars in Marketing and Advertising. What's the use of a great product if there's no one to buy and use it? Imagine if the iPhone wasn't properly and strategically promoted, Apple won't have the enormous profit they have today and most us of will certainly miss out on such an amazing device. The principle holds true whether it's a small or big business - Marketing is essential to its short and long term success.

It All Starts with A Plan

Most businesses fail simply because they don't have a marketing plan. Many think a business plan is the only thing needed. Nothing can be more misleading. Even soldiers on a battlefield have a strategic plan. Every business needs a marketing plan no matter how simple.

Your marketing plan doesn't have to be something as complex and complicated as a business plan. A simple and comprehensive plan will do just fine. Although a plan doesn't give you any surefire guarantee, you can't do much without it either.

A Quick 5-Point Draft
Here's a 5-point guideline to help you;

1. Clearly define your business scope (what specific area(s) will you focus your marketing efforts? New products or new markets? etc.)
2. Define your unique proposition (what are you really selling? What makes your offer compelling and unique? Brand Strength etc.)
3. Customer Focus (who's your ideal customer/target audience? Their Location – online or local? etc.)
4. Define your strategy (Determine your Budget, What mediums will you employ to promote your business – Social media, Magazines, TV? How do you attract, Serve and Keep your customers? How do you plan to deal with competition? etc.)

5. Define your Marketing Goals and Result Measurement Criteria (20% sales increase, increased repeat customer ratio? Increased market presence etc.)

You can draft a quick marketing plan with the guidelines above and be sure to improve it as you grow and learn more.

Start Now!

One of the excuses many entrepreneurs give for not doing much marketing for their businesses is that they feel they don't know enough about marketing, they're not ready yet or they don't have enough money. But the truth is that you don't need to know all about marketing. You can start right now. Reading this book is an important step in the right direction. You don't need to be a Marketing and Sales Guru before you start marketing your business to improve your Sales. All you need is an open mind and be willing to learn along the way.

Smart Thoughts

- Marketing is the processes and means businesses employ to create value for customers in form of a unique offering that meets their needs so as to capture value back from the customers.
- Marketing is about Relationships. You're in a relationship with customers – to create and deliver Value for and to them.
- Marketing is very important to the success of your business both in the short and long terms.
- Your marketing plan doesn't have to be something as complex and complicated as a business plan. A simple plan will do just fine.
- You don't need to be a Marketing and Sales Guru before you start marketing your business.... All you

need is to have an open mind and be willing to learn along the way.

2. YOUR UNIQUE VALUE PROPOSITION

Why should I do business with you right now rather than buy from the other store that's running a discount week? What's special about you? Getting answers to these questions helps you define and capture what your Unique Value Proposition is. Having identified this quality that makes you stand out, you'll then proceed to incorporate it into your entire business. We'll discuss this in detail in this chapter.

Defining Your Unique Value Proposition

As you set out in the process of Marketing, you need to clearly define and understand your unique value proposition so as to make the most of your marketing efforts.

To do this, take a moment and consider the following:

- What makes your offering special?
- Can you deliver your offering in a way others can't?

- What benefits do your offer provides that others don't?
- How can you leverage those advantages?
- Can you deliver your service faster, cheaper and more efficiently than others?
- Can you offer a guarantee?

What Are You Really Selling?

This is probably the most important question you need to ask yourself in business. It's actually a two-fold question.

First, you should ask yourself "What am I offering that others can't?" Secondly, "What advantage do I have with customers that others in the same business don't?" The first part of the question deals with your Unique Value Proposition. The second part then is about describing your Competitive Advantage. Think about these things until you come up with clear answers.

For instance, if you're a fashion designer, you might be able to sew good clothes for customers in a very distant place because you don't need to meet with or take measurements of them before you do make their clothes. Now that's a unique advantage. Many of your competitors won't be able to beat that.

These questions are very important when it comes to crafting a successful Marketing Strategy. You must identify your uniqueness early, as clearly as possible and make sure you build your marketing strategy around it!

Smart idea: Build your marketing strategy around your unique proposition.

Here's another Practical Example. Mike is a Clothier. He makes affordable and quality corporate uniforms and work clothes of all kinds for his customers. What does he sell? You say Clothes, that's correct. But what does he really sell that makes him different? Affordable and quality Corporate Uniforms and Work Clothes of all kinds. Gotcha! So this makes it easier for Mike to get Customers because he doesn't just make the kind of clothes every other clothier does.

Second, let's assume Mike has a good designing ability coupled with his sewing skill. He could make a quick sketch and design for the client on his first engagement. When he does this, the client has a vivid image of what the clothes will look like and he's more likely to do business with Mike. This little advantage gives Mike a tremendous edge over other designers.

He's carved a niche for himself. He has a specific and clear work focus. He has a competitive advantage. This is what separates him from the competition. You see, a good marketing strategy sets you apart from the pack. It gives you a distinct opportunity of sales. In Mike's case, if you need just about any cloth, you might as well walk up to any clothier around you. But if you need a clothier that makes affordable and quality Corporate Uniforms and Work Clothes, chances are you will look for Mike and give him the job.

Smart Idea: A good marketing strategy sets you apart from the pack.

Who's Your Ideal Customer? (Market)
There's nothing more frustrating than a product or service that no one needs. Another important question to ask yourself is "Who is my ideal customer?", "who needs what I'm producing?"

Be as clear and specific as possible. For instance, in Mike's case, it'll include new businesses that need a corporate uniform or work apparel and even already established businesses that want to redesign their uniforms or rebrand their staff. This will more precisely include startups, banks, schools and other organizations. Although we'll discuss Customers in detail in the next chapter, it's important to state here that if there's no specific target customer for your business; your chances of success are very slim. In fact, failure is almost predictable.

Is It Worth It? (Value)

In business, you basically get paid for the Value you provide. The third question you need to ask yourself then is "is the product or service I'm offering worth paying for?", "Does my business solve a problem?", "am I meeting a need?", "can people do without my product or service?"

Asking these questions will help you capture the value of your offering with more clarity. You'll see beyond just the activity of selling to your customers. You'll connect with them on a deeper level. You'll be doing them some 'good'. Imagine your customers thanking you after making a purchase!

Believe me, if you're not offering any Value in your product or service, if people don't feel what you're selling them is worth it, you'll soon be out of business. So take some time and get the answers to these questions.

Differentiate: Don't Be Among "The Many"

The essence of all the discussions in those last pages is to ultimately empower you to differentiate yourself and your business from the "many". You'll agree with me that there seem to be new businesses every now and then. Almost every fine-looking young man out there is an entrepreneur of some sort (no offense). So, the most effective way, in fact, the only way to thrive in today's marketplace is to be unique.

The most expensive mistake businesses, especially small ones make is not being unique. It bears repeating – You must be unique. No matter the business you're in; Consulting, Sales, Retail, whatever it is you do, your success is in your uniqueness.

Some might ask "why should I be unique?" It's simple - because you don't want to be among the "many businesses". Why? Because many businesses fail!

How Do You Become Unique?

The best way to be unique is by Identifying, developing, and incorporating your **Unique Value Proposition** into everything you do. It will differentiate you, distinguish you, and give you advantage over everyone else in your marketplace.

You see, "Me too" businesses rarely survive. They usually end up in price-wars because they don't have any uniqueness to differentiate them in the mind of the customers. This is a very dangerous position.

Another reason you should be unique is that the more unique you are the more customers will be able to recognize and ultimately choose you above your competitors. To know whether you're unique or not, when a customer thinks about products or services in your industry, is your name in the Top 3 that comes to mind? (Don't be naïve; of course there are other factors that'll determine your 'reputation' in the market. But your uniqueness is very important. Think about APPLE for a moment!)

"Me too" businesses rarely survive.

Having identified your UVP, the next thing to do is integrate it into every part of your business. It should reflect in your tagline, your service delivery and culture. This way, it then becomes your **Unique Selling Proposition**. Your USP further stands you out in the marketplace, even in the entire industry.

There are some important elements of a good USP. It should include:
- A specific promise of some kind (Close-Up's "Deep fresh breath" tagline).
- A specific service expectation (Domino's Pizza's "A fresh, hot pizza delivered in 30 minutes or less, guaranteed").
- A specific guarantee (Have a look at Duracell battery's tagline).
- Specific Customer/Industry focus especially for service-based businesses (A Graphic/Website Designer that focuses on E-commerce websites for Retail stores).

You get the idea? So, just get to work and let the creative juice flow!

Let me add something important at this point since we're talking about Unique Value Proposition: during a depression, recession or a general economic downturn, while everyone else is focusing on beating prices and cutting costs, it is wise to introduce Creative and Value-added Offers that further enhance your uniqueness and encourage people to do business with you. You don't necessarily have to announce to people that you're trying to "help". No one will do business with you because you show sympathy. Rather, focus on delivering the maximum value possible for every penny a customer invests in doing business with you.

Smart Thoughts

- You need to clearly define and understand your unique value proposition so as to make the most of your marketing efforts.
- You must identify your uniqueness early, as clearly as possible and make sure you build your marketing strategy around it!
- The most expensive mistake businesses, especially small ones make is not being unique. The best way to be unique is by Identifying, developing, and incorporating your **Unique Value Proposition (UVP)** into everything you do.

- The UVP and USP are the most important elements of Marketing.

3. CUSTOMERS

Marketing is really about "more". More sales, more customers, more profits, more market share just name it. If you get everything else right but your marketing is wrong, you still wouldn't get the results you should.

If I can summarize this entire section in a single statement it will be this: **Marketing, business in a bigger picture, is about Making and Selling the Right Product or Service to the Right Person – the Customer**. This is essentially true in business because selling to the right person is more important than all the sales methods and tactics in the world. And it follows that nothing else in business can make up for poor marketing – not schemes or gimmicks, not brand building or even heavy advertising.

Marketing is also about Problem-solving. The best marketing strategies create solutions for the customer. My ultimate marketing formula is this:

CUSTOMER ⟹ PRODUCT/SERVICE

As you can easily understand, the illustration simply describes the marketing process: The Customer First, then the product or service you're offering. Some "experts" advices that you build a product then you go looking for whom to sell it. We've seen time and again that this doesn't work, at least, as it used to. The best way to go about this is to create a specific offering to address specific customer needs. Understanding this simple principle will save you a great deal of time and energy often spent doing marketing the wrong way.

Earlier, I said something about selling to the right person, the customer. Then you ask, how do I identify the right person?

It's simple –

- The right person needs your product/service.
- He has the money to pay for it.
- You can actually reach him or her in some way that's not too difficult.

- You won't need to spend an entire day persuading them to do business with you (in most cases).

It's All About The Customer

It is the norm in some businesses to often find staff or employees regarding and treating business-owners and bosses as the most important stakeholders. The respect and care they are shown sometimes at the expense of good customer service amazes me. What most people don't know is that one of the reasons all business organizations exist is to serve the customer.

Customers are the most important stakeholders in any business. The rule is simple: No customer no business! Of course, businesses should cater for employees and management; this shouldn't be done at the expense of good customer service.

One of the challenges in contemporary business is attracting, satisfying and retaining customers, especially for new and small businesses. But then, in this age and time that we live in, nothing can be simpler. Note I said Simpler; attracting customers can be quite simple these days but not necessarily easy. All you need is to be Creative. The rule bears repeating: No customers, No business. Can you imagine banking halls with no customers, just the staff doing stuffs on their computers? It's unthinkable. The best businesses are those that attract, satisfy and retain customers. It is important that I mention here that the best businesses are those that are built around Customers. The customer has to be at the center of your business model.

Types of Customers

Writers and marketing enthusiasts have categorized customers into several types. In fact, there as many types of customers as there are several types marketing. In this book, I'll briefly discuss the types of customers from a sales-oriented perspective.

1. The Prospect

A prospect is anyone who has shown interest in your product or service. It could be by singing up for your newsletters, reading your book or any other free resource you give out. They are also usually referred to as the potential customer. You need to show them the value you have to offer and engage them appropriately.

2. The New Customer

This is anyone who just made a purchase of your product or service. You actually had a transaction with them. You need to invest some time to build a good relationship with them and keep your communication channels with them open.

3. The Impulsive Customer

These are customers that purchase your products based on their impulses. While they're not necessarily persuaded by your marketing, they just can't seem to resist your offer. You need to provide a smooth purchase and payment channel to really satisfy this customer.

4. The Discount Customer

These kinds of customers are often looking for product and services with discounts. They always want that little extra offer. They often buy low-cost products. For this customer, you need to take your time to explain the deal and offer value-added services.

5. The Loyal Customer

The loyal customer usually keeps coming back to your business for more. These are the ones every business wish they have more of. This is because the more loyal customers your business has, the more successful you'll likely be. They are like your fans and they can easily tell others about your business. However, they are usually very less in number than the other types of customers. Bulk of your revenue will come from these because of the repeat sales.

These kinds of customers usually demand personal attention and care. You need to really involve and engage them often. You need to learn from them to understand how they became loyal customers so you can apply the knowledge to bring other customers to the same level. Ultimately, you should never disappoint them. And when you do, be sure to do all you can to win back their trust.

Even with the several types and categories of customers, they all have one thing in common – the desire for a value that satisfies and they can pay for.

How well do you know your customers?

If I asked you to tell me five things about your customers, would you be able to? Of course you should, and more. Do you know that the most successful businesses in this century know as much as there is to know about their customers? So why shouldn't you? Can I add that the bulk of customer knowledge that top companies like Apple, Google and Amazon has contributes so much to their financial success?

Any business that will maximize its marketing efforts must know as much as it can about the customers it serves.

In fact, you should know –
- Who buys
- What they buy
- How they buy
- When they buy
- Where they are comfortable buying
- What they earn
- What they'll likely buy
- Other basic and useful information about them.

Knowing as much as you can about your customers will not only help you tailor your offerings strategically, it'll also get you a step ahead of your competitors. While your competitors are still anticipating and guessing customers' needs, you'll already know them.

Attracting Customers

Attracting customers can be quite challenging but it's not rocket science. I bet if you take a minute right now and think of a new way to attract new customers to your business you'll definitely come up with one.

Here are some ideas to help you:

Create a Good Product

No greater strategy than this. Build a great product that can almost sell itself. It starts with finding out what the customer needs and producing it in a cost-effective manner. Then you can proceed to market your business with few struggles and cajoling. Remember, no amount of Marketing can make up for a poor product.

Word-of-mouth (The Classic)

This is a time-tested and proven strategy that works every single time. It still emphasizes the first point - build a great product that people can't help but talk about. And you should encourage your customers to "tell others" about your product or service. If your service is really good, they sure will.

Use Social Media

The internet is the primary marketplace today with billions of transaction done daily. Have a standard website if you need one and be active on appropriate Social Networks. Invest in Digital marketers or learn how to promote your business online yourself. Also, make a full description of your business on your social media pages. Encourage your friends and followers to do business with you, repost and share your promotional contents. More on digital marketing later.

Offer a Free Product
It still works! Who doesn't like "Free"? Use discounts and Coupons wisely too. Just make sure you offer something valuable not just something anyone can get anywhere for next to nothing. You can also use the world-famous "Freemium" strategy – offer free value to get prospects to pay for premium contents.

Use the 'Test-drive' Strategy
A story is told of a car dealer who increased his sales by offering test-drives in strategic places like beaches and malls. You can try it too if your product or service can be "tried". Be sure to target likely prospects not just someone that'll try your product but can't afford it.

Do "Seasonal" Sales
It started with the big names in online retail like Alibaba but many Nigerian brands now use the

same strategy. Leverage on unique seasons and events to promote your business. You can have a World cup sales promotion, Christmas Sales offer, New Year discounts, Back-to-school Sales promo, Black Friday etc. The list is endless. Just get creative.

Referrals

This is one of the most effective marketing channels. In fact, it is often underutilized. Do your best to provide a very good product or deliver your service in a remarkable way. Then politely encourage your customers to recommend you for business. I'm sure they will.

You can learn and apply these simple ideas to help you get new clients and more business as a result.

Smart Idea: while a satisfied customer tells one person about your business an unsatisfied customer tells nine!

Satisfying Customers

While many businesses succeed at attracting customers, some fail at satisfying them. To satisfy customers, you need to go the extra mile. While it's impossible to satisfy all your customers (and you shouldn't cos that'll be suicide), you can focus on practices that can satisfy most of them. Here's something you should know: while a satisfied customer tells one person about your business an unsatisfied customer tells nine!

Here are some suggestions to help you get started in satisfying your customers:

Make them Feel Important

Why? Because they are! Moreover, who doesn't like to be treated like a VIP? So, at every chance you get, make your customer feel like the most important person in the world at that moment and they'll leave satisfied and happy. You can do this by giving them your time, undivided attention and focus.

Care for their Kids

Oh this is one of the most important ideas many businesses ignore (and that to their own loss). Make your business environment so comfortable that your customers don't have to worry about their kids when they do business with you. You can have a little playground and toys if you have enough space. Do this and you'll see your sales skyrocket.

Have a Standard Convenience System

Can you imagine how many businesses lose customers because they don't have a good restroom? If there's a way you can have a nice, clean and well-maintained restroom in your business, I advise that you do so urgently. Trust me, it'll increase your patronage more than you expect. The idea is to make your customers feel as comfortable as they can while doing business with you.

Smart idea: Be nice to your Competitor's Customer.

Make Payment System Easy

You can lose customers if you make it difficult for customers to **PAY** you. Can you imagine a restaurant in this century that doesn't have a POS? Have as many payment options as possible for easy and convenient transactions.

Listen

This is an important part of customer engagement. It's by far the most efficient way to get a customer's attention and get them to tell you their needs. Learn to practice good, focused and "I'm-right-here-with-you" listening. Who doesn't like to be listened to? I know I do. Don't get distracted while having a conversation with a customer. Don't try to attend to the customer in the phone while there's someone standing before you. Listen for emotional cues, pay attention to their body language, just focus on them for the moment. Truly care. You won't only understand what they need when you do this, they'll also be glad to do business with you.

Engage

Engage your customers as often as possible. You can have simple and casual conversations with them, get to know them better so you can ultimately understand and satisfy their needs.

Focus on Customers' Needs

Successful businesses know that customers' needs come first. This is simply the desire or motive that prompts a customer to purchase a product or service. When you put the customers' needs first, you position your business for success both in the short and long terms because human needs don't change, they evolve. Apparently, our basic need for food, shelter and safety hasn't changed at all.

Retaining Customers

This is another very important aspect of marketing in business. This is because the biggest share of the profits you'll make will most likely come from repeat sales, customers that come back.

Here's a few tips to help you keep customers:

Great Customer Service

This is a sure way to keep customers and make them come back to do business with you. Deliver your service in the best way possible - faster, cheaper and better.

Ask for Feedbacks

Always ask for and respond to feedbacks and improvement suggestions from customers. As much as you can, be available to attend to after-sales and support requests promptly. Respond to social media suggestions and comments from customers. Remember to thank them when they give their honest opinions too.

Keep a Record

Try as much as you can to get the most important details on your Customers – their favorite things and places, Birthdays, Wedding anniversaries etc. Call or text them on special occasions, you should even send a greeting card when you can. This will make them feel truly special.

Stay in Touch

Have a phone number directory and put a call through every once in a while. Please don't call too often. And make it warm, brief and straight-to-the-point (Check up on them and maybe tell them about a new product). You can also use newsletters to keep your customers updated on your newest products and sales offers.

A word on Customer Relationship

Businesses need to continually interact with customers. A good and healthy customer relationship is established when both parties diverge from s state of autonomy to mutual or interdependent. Successful companies understand and take advantage of this.

Customer relationship has two basic dimensions which is the ultimate goal of building a relationship with the customer - Trust and Commitment.

Trust is established when the customer becomes intimate with products and services a company offers and even with the company itself. It is when all doubts and risks are minimized on both sides.

Commitment is achieved when the relationship between a company and a customer has evolved such that there is mutual trust and shared values. The customers become really loyal to the company at this point that the relationship can be compared to that of a cult. Very few companies can attain this level of customer relationship but it is a goal worth working towards.

Smart Thoughts

- Marketing, business in a bigger picture, is about Making and Selling the Right Product or Service to the Right Person – the Customer.
- Selling to the right person is more important than all the sales methods and tactics in the world.
- Any business that will maximize its marketing efforts must know as much as it can about the customers it serves.

- It's important that you learn how to attract, satisfy and retain customers.
- While a satisfied customer tells one person about your business an unsatisfied customer tells nine!
- Customer relationship has two basic dimensions which is the ultimate goal of building a relationship with the customer - Trust and Commitment.

4. THE MARKETING EDGE

Earlier in this book, I noted that marketing isn't and should never be a one-time event, rather, it should be a part of your everyday business practice. Some business-owners do some small marketing at the outset but when sales increases they stop. They get caught up "working in" their business that they forget to "work on" it. If there's something you must take away from this book it's this: Don't ever stop "working on" your business.

To achieve enduring business success, you need learn to make marketing an integral part of your business. It gives you a tremendous advantage over others. This is what I often describe as **"The Marketing Edge"**. I describe it this way because so many entrepreneurs only think of marketing when they're starting out or when sales nosedive. Even worse, some depend on fate and luck. This is often the reason some businesses get entangled in price wars and all sorts of sales gimmicks.

On the other hand, the ones that make marketing and promoting their businesses a habit tend to do better. They get consistent results. To do this, I'd suggest you schedule at least three marketing activities into your daily work routine. Try to do at least three things that promote your business every single day. It could be dedicating two hours of study to understand new trends in your industry to improve your business, posting quality contents on social networks or talking to old customers and asking for feedbacks.

Invest in Digital Marketing

It is important to leverage the overwhelming opportunities that exist online these days. It's always wise to outsource some functions like social media marketing to professionals because you can't do everything yourself. Also, there are various courses and books available online that can help if you want to learn how to do this yourself.

Here are a few things to try:

- Building a Blog that engages your audience.
- Email Marketing.
- Video: Leveraging the second largest search engine in the World.
- Content Marketing: Infographics, Videos.
- Building a Presence on Twitter, Facebook, Google+, and other social networks.
- Use social media influencers.

Adopt Quality Promotional Materials.

You need people, especially your customers, to perceive your business as excellent and Top-notch. This is why branding yourself and your company properly is so important. Invest in high quality promotional contents, Top-notch Graphics Design and all other things you need. Having quality branding materials presents you before your audience as someone they can do business with. There's an important principle I learnt in business a long time ago; if you want people to do business with you, you need to dress, look and present yourself like those they already do business with.

Don't stop Improving your Product/Service.

This is really important. If you have a great product this year and you fail to improve and innovate, either your competitors will soon catch up with you or your product becomes obsolete before the next year. Do you remember the Sony Walkman? Yahoo Messenger? I'm sure you understand what happened to them - they became obsolete.

Find out new and better ways to create and deliver your value. Try new things often. Read good books on subjects in your industry, attend seminars, trainings and workshops, just keep learning and improving your greatest asset - You.

Leverage Your Strengths.

You don't have to worry about every single detail in running your business. You can hire professionals to help you in areas you're not very good at. Most people, especially Africans don't do this because they feel it's a waste of time and resources. But it's not true. The most successful business people know they can't do everything. They outsource things outside their area of competence so they can focus on what they know how to do best. Some outsource their Marketing, Product development, Customer service to outsiders so they can have enough time to focus on and get better at their core competencies. This is certainly the wisest thing to do in today's complex and complicated business environment simply because you don't have unlimited time and energy. So learn to scale by leveraging your strengths.

Getting the Best Returns on Your Ads and Marketing Campaigns

To get the best returns on your investment in a marketing campaign or advertisement, I recommend the following:
Focus on a specific objective
Instead of just doing marketing for marketing's sake, focus each campaign or advertisement on a specific objective. You need to set clear goals so you can determine which

platforms to focus on. For instance, do you want to create awareness for a specific product, drive traffic to your website or build your social media audience? Start by establishing an objective then structure your ads or campaign to achieve this. Don't just do your marketing haphazardly. Have a goal and let it direct your marketing efforts.

Communicate one simple Message at a time

Many ads don't yield the results expected because we often try to communicate too many messages in a single campaign. We want the customer to buy products A, B and C, visit the store then follow us on Instagram and Twitter, all in a single ad? Come on, you're marketing to humans not robots. You should never forget that most people, especially those you're marketing to find it difficult to "remember". Humans have short attention span. Our ability to actually pay attention is rapidly declining. Do you know that the average adult is exposed to about a hundred thousand words daily? Elevator pitches don't even seem to work anymore as we're all busy with our phones texting or replying mails even in the elevator. Trying to kill two birds with a stone doesn't work here. Make your ads as smart, precise, and memorable as possible.

Sell the benefits

Let your adverts and campaigns emphasize the benefits of your offering not just how much of an expert you are. They don't really care that much.

Include a direct Call-to-Action

Don't tell people to send you an email, DM you on Instagram, call a number and text you just to purchase a product. Apologies if it seems like I overemphasized that. I hope you get the point. Don't make it too complex and difficult for your customers to communicate with you either. In essence, don't clutter your ads with too many details, just focus on what's necessary to bring the sale home. Here, less really is more and simple is better.

Measure results

This is why it's important to set clear marketing objectives right from the beginning. You need to measure the results you're getting in-line with the goals and objectives already established. This would help you to know which platforms work for you and which ones don't. You'll be able to readjust your strategies accordingly.

Smart Thoughts

- Marketing isn't and should never be a one-time event, rather, it should be a part of your everyday business practice.
- Schedule at least three marketing activities into your daily routine.
- If you want people to do business with you, dress, look and present yourself like those they already do business with.
- Find out new and better ways to deliver the value you create.
- Learn to scale by leveraging your strengths.
- Trying to kill two birds with a stone doesn't work here. Make your ads as smart, precise, and memorable as possible.
- Don't clutter your ads with too many details, just focus on what's necessary to bring the sale home. Here, less really is more and simple is better.

FINAL WORDS

Well done! You've finally reached the end of the book. I bet you're smarter now than you were at the beginning. I hope you see some major changes in how you view and do your marketing, relate with your customers and work on your business.

Don't Stop Here

I'm learning every day and continually improving myself. I hope you are too. I learn new things and get better every time I help a client improve their business. I hope you also understand that no one becomes a pro at anything by just reading a book. It takes consistent practice. With that, you'll get there sooner than you expect. Every worthwhile endeavors takes time to attain. Keep working on yourself and your business, you'll be glad you did.

Get Started

Remember, Life doesn't reward you for what you know, no, you only get paid and applauded for what you DO! Don't wait for the perfect time, just get out there and Do something. You don't have to be one hundred percent ready or be an expert to begin. Just start! And you'll be amazed at the results you'll get. The most important thing isn't what you know when you're starting but what you can learn on the way

I'd love to help!

I'm passionate about helping businesses but even more, I'm passionate about helping others lead their best lives and fully express their personal Leadership. Please leave your comments and suggestions on my blog www.damilarefakorede.com and kindly drop a review on Amazon if you love this book. Be sure to recommend it to friends and family who might need it.

If you have questions or you ever get stuck, don't hesitate to give me a shout! You can always contact me via the information in the **Author's Bio** section below.

AUTHOR'S BIO

Damilare is a Business Consultant, Author, Leadership and Personal Development Coach. He's the Co-founder of ICI Consulting.

His passion is evident in his drive to add value to startups and already established businesses especially in areas like Marketing and Sales Improvement, Branding and Leadership Development. All this he does with a penchant for excellence. With a creative and calculated manner of approach, it's no wonder Damilare produces consistent results always.

Connect with Damilare:
Instagram - @darefakorede
Twitter - @darefakorede
LinkedIn - Damilare Fakorede
Email - darefakorede@gmail.com

ABOUT ICI

ICI Consulting is a management consulting firm that provides Valuable Performance-driven, and Creative Business and Leadership Solutions to individuals and organizations.

Our Management Consulting practice currently includes: Business Model Analysis and Development, Strategy, Sales and Marketing, Branding and Leadership Development.

Send us an email to book a session today.

Email - iciconsultingng@gmail.com

Mobile - +2348140092551

www.ingramcontent.com/pod-product-compliance
Lightning Source LLC
Chambersburg PA
CBHW021511210526
45463CB00002B/976